KIDS' COOKBOOK 2

MURDOCH BOOKS

Sydney • London • Vancouver

The Publisher thanks the following for their assistance:

Accoutrement Cookshops
Barbara's Storehouse
Bisana Tiles
Corso De' Fiori
Domus Tiles
Grace Bros
Home & Garden on the Mall

All recipes in this book can be made by
a child with little or no help from an adult.
All the microwave recipes have been
tested in a 600-700 watt microwave.
Each recipe is set out to make cooking
simple.

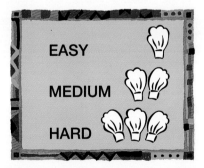

EASY

MEDIUM

HARD

Recipes are graded to help you learn. If
you are just starting out to cook you
might prefer to try the recipes marked
easy (one chef's hat); when you have a
little experience, try medium (two chefs'
hats) and when you are more exper-
ienced try the harder recipes marked by
three chefs' hats.

CONTENTS

Cooking is great fun and we've made it easy with our step-by-step recipes. Before you start, take time to get organised. Choose your recipe and read it all the way through, then check that you have all the ingredients. Collect everything you are going to use — all the ingredients and all the equipment.

If your recipe calls for chopped or shredded ingredients, do this before you begin. Also, open any cans and wash any vegetables or fruit. Grease any baking tins or microwave cookware if you need to.

If you need to use the oven for baking, turn it on to the correct temperature before you start the recipe. Arrange the oven shelves at the height you want before turning the oven on.

Before you start cooking in the microwave, read over our microwave section on page 11 to learn about the special methods and equipment that you need to know to make every recipe a success.

All the recipes are set out with step-by-step pictures so they are very easy to follow. Remember to finish each step before beginning the next one.

When you have finished cooking, clean up the kitchen. Put away all the ingredients and the equipment you have used. Wash the dishes — start with washing the least dirty dishes and then work up to the really messy pans. Dry dishes and put them back in their place. Wipe down your work surface with a clean cloth and then, I'm sure, you'll be allowed to cook again another day.

IMPORTANT SAFETY RULES

Here are a few hints and tips to make cooking safe and enjoyable.

✔ Always ask an adult for permission before you start.

✔ Before starting to cook, wash your hands well with soap and water. Wear an apron to protect your clothes and wear closed-in, non-slippery shoes to protect your feet.

✔ Unless you are allowed to use knives, ask an adult to help you chop things. Never cut directly on a kitchen bench or table — always use a chopping board. Pick knives up by the handle, not the blade. Keep fingers well clear when chopping foods.

✔ Take care when washing knives, too. Keep the sharp edge of the blade away from you and store the knives out of reach of any younger brothers or sisters.

✔ Always use oven mitts to remove anything from the oven or microwave. Also remember that anything you take from the top of the stove or the oven will stay hot for a while.

✔ Be very careful with pots and pans on the stove. Never reach across a hot saucepan — steam is very hot and can cause a nasty scald.

✔ Turn saucepan handles to the side when cooking so you don't knock them. Hold the handles of saucepans when stirring foods on the stove so that the pan won't slip. Use a wooden spoon — metal spoons can get hot when stirring hot foods.

✔ Place hot saucepans and ovenproof dishes on a chopping board when you take them from the oven or the stove. Never set a hot pan directly on the kitchen bench or table, unless it is covered with ceramic tiles.

✔ Don't put your fingers into hot pans or mixtures.

✔ Never use electrical appliances near water. Always have dry hands before you start to use any appliance.

✔ Remember to turn off the oven, the hotplate or gas ring or any other appliance when you have finished using it.

FIRST AID BURNS AND SCALDS

If you should burn or scald yourself, cool down the burn with cold water for 10 minutes (hold it under the cold tap). Protect against infection by gently covering the burn or scald with a clean, non-sticking bandage. Do not touch the burn.

COOK'S TOOLS

The recipes in this book use the basic equipment found in most kitchens. If in doubt about any equipment you may need, ask an adult for some help.

There are many tools used in the kitchen to make cooking easy. There are wooden and metal spoons to stir with, spatulas to combine ingredients, bowls of varying sizes to mix things in, strainers or colanders to drain and rinse foods in, and a whole array of saucepans and baking trays to cook things in. There are wire racks for cooling cakes and cookies, metal spatulas to help you measure and also to spread toppings evenly over food.

SOME COOKING TERMS

BEAT: To stir foods with a spoon or electric mixer until they are smooth.

BOILING POINT: When a liquid bubbles in a steady pattern and the bubbles break on the surface. Steam also starts to rise from the pan.

CHOP: Cut food carefully into small pieces. To chop finely is to cut foods as small as you can.

DRAIN: To strain away unwanted liquid from rice, pasta or vegetables using a colander or strainer. Do this over the kitchen sink so that water can drain away down the sink. OR fried foods need to be drained sometimes. Lift food out of frypan and place on brown paper or paper towels to absorb the extra oil or fat.

GRATE: To rub food against a grater. Do this over absorbent paper. Hold the grater with one hand and rub the food back and forth over the grating holes. This gives you long, thin pieces. For finely grated food, use the smallest holes.

GREASE: To rub baking tins and cooking utensils with butter, margarine or oil to stop foods sticking when you bake them.

KNEAD: Lightly rub and roll foods like pastry or scone dough on a floured surface until smooth and pliable.

MASH: To squash cooked or very ripe foods with a fork or potato masher to make a soft mixture.

SEPARATING EGGS: When egg whites or yolks are needed for a recipe. Hold the egg over a small plate and carefully crack the shell with a knife. Let the egg fall out onto the plate, place a small glass over the yolk and then carefully tip the white into a bowl. If any yolk gets into the white, you can easily remove it with a piece of eggshell.

SIMMER: To cook food over a very low heat, so that only a few bubbles appear over the surface. When a recipe calls for food to boil and then simmer, simply turn the heat down to the lowest setting.

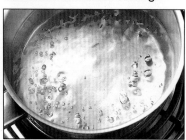

SLICE: To cut foods such as apples, carrots or tomatoes into thin rounds or sections.

WHISK: To mix ingredients together with a balloon-shaped, wire mixer (a whisk) by moving in a circular motion until smooth or combined.

MEASURING UP

Careful measuring of ingredients makes for a successful recipe. You will need a set of dry measuring cups, which usually come in a set of four: 1 cup, ½ cup, ⅓ cup and ¼ cup measures. These are used to measure ingredients such as flour and sugar. You will also need a liquid measuring cup that usually has a lip for easy pouring and lines on the side that mark the different liquid measures. Milk, cream, water and juice are measured with this cup. Measuring spoons will also be needed to measure small amounts. They are marked and measure
1 tablespoon, 1 teaspoon,
½ teaspoon and ¼ teaspoon.

DRY MEASURES

Take care to use the correct size measuring cup as stated in the recipe, especially if you are baking cakes or cookies. Spoon the dry ingredients lightly into the measuring cup and level it off with a spatula. It's a good idea to do this over a piece of absorbent paper to avoid any mess.

In some recipes you will need to do some simple maths to get the correct amount you need. For example, you may need ⅔ cup flour for a recipe, so simply measure out ⅓ cup using the correct measure and then another ⅓ cup and add both to the recipe.

LIQUID MEASURES

To measure a liquid place the measuring cup on the bench or board, add some of the liquid and bend down so that your eyes are level with the measurement marks. Check to see if you have enough liquid; if necessary, pour in more. If you have too much, simply pour out the extra.

SPOON MEASURES

Measuring spoons are different from the spoons you use for eating. They are used to measure small amounts.

To measure liquids, choose the correct size spoon for the amount you need and carefully pour the liquid into the spoon.

BUTTER

Butter is generally measured in grams. You will find that blocks of butter have a weight marking on the side of the wrapper. Use a small knife to cut through the butter at the correct marking and then unwrap it. Butter can also be weighed using a kitchen scale.

It's a good idea to hold the spoon over a cup or jug to avoid spills.

To measure dry ingredients, fill the correct size spoon with dry ingredients and then carefully level off the top with a metal spatula.

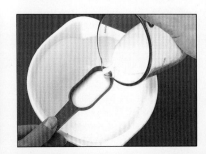

MICROWAVE KNOW HOW

Microwave cooking is great fun, too. Before you start, read this page to learn the special techniques and equipment you need to make your recipes a success.

All microwave ovens are different. Before beginning to cook get to know a little about your microwave oven. You may need to ask an adult to help you.

• Firstly, find out what wattage your microwave oven is — this is important to determine cooking times. All our recipes were tested in a 600-700 watt microwave. If yours has fewer watts, foods will take a little longer to cook.

• Learn how to operate or set your microwave oven from High to Low and how to set the timer.

• Here are the temperatures and percentages we used:

High: 100% power
Medium/High: 75% power
Medium: 50% power
Low: 30% power

• Some foods cook a little more quickly than others in a particular dish. These foods need stirring as they cook, so that they cook evenly.

• Place microwave dishes in the centre of the microwave oven.

MICROWAVE CONTAINERS

• Lots of special microwave containers are made out of plastic. Before you use them, look underneath the dish to make sure it tells you how it can be used. Some say they are suitable for most things but not for foods with lots of fat, oil or sugar. These get very, very, hot and if you're not using a suitable plastic dish, the heat could damage it or even make it melt!

• Don't use any metal containers in the microwave.

• Don't use any dishes, plates, mugs or cups that have a silver or gold trim. These metals react badly with microwaves. The nice trim could turn a nasty colour, or more important, it may cause sparks that could damage the oven.

• Don't use fine bone china, crystal bowls or glasses.

• Some pottery mugs or casserole dishes have a glaze that contains small amounts of metal. These can get very hot in the microwave and could give you a nasty burn — check with an adult before using if you're not sure.

• The best containers to use, especially for cooking with liquid, are those with a handle for safe removal from the microwave. Don't forget — the oven might feel cool, but the dish could be hot, so have some oven mitts ready.

MICROWAVE COOK'S TOOLS

Microwave cooking requires some specially-made equipment, because ordinary pans and dishes can damage the microwave. There are wooden and micro-safe spoons to stir with, racks to elevate dishes in the oven and micro-safe dishes to cook things in.

MICROWAVE SAFETY POINTS

✔ Always use oven mitts to remove anything from the microwave. Remember that anything you take from the microwave oven will be hot for a while.

✔ When you uncover foods just out of the microwave take great care that the steam doesn't burn you. Lift the far side of the cover up first, letting the steam go up and out away from you.

✔ When stirring microwave dishes, hold the container with oven mitts as you stir.

✔ Never operate the microwave oven without food inside.

✔ Never put anything made of metal into the microwave.

MICROWAVE COOKING TERMS

COVER: Make sure you do "cover" when the recipe tells you to or food might dry out. But also, don't forget to leave off the lid or cling wrap when the recipe says "cook uncovered". If you leave a cover on when it should not be, it could cause the food to boil over.

GREASE: To brush micro containers and cooking utensils with melted butter or oil to stop foods sticking.

PIERCE: This is when you make holes in the cling wrap cover in several places with a fork to avoid liquid boiling over.

RACKS: These are used for lifting dishes up a little from the bottom of the microwave oven. It helps cakes and some desserts to cook more evenly. If you don't have a rack, you can use a small, upturned saucer or dish.

STIR: We say this a lot when microwaving, because if you don't stir the food or liquid regularly, the outside of the food gets hot while the middle is only slightly warm.

CHAPTER ONE

Here's some quick and easy dishes to make when hunger strikes and there's no time to wait. Some are hot and tasty to warm up a winter afternoon; in summer, cool down with a Fruity Yoghurt Pop. Whatever the weather, you'll enjoy these snacks all year round.

HOT BEAN DOGS

Makes 4

4 continental frankfurts
4 hot dog rolls
120 g butter
225 g can baked beans
  in tomato sauce
4 tablespoons coarsely
  grated Cheddar cheese
4 tablespoons sweet
  mustard

Cut 5 slits into each frankfurt.

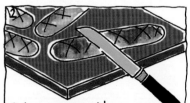

Cut 5 more slits across the first to make a pattern.

Put franks under hot grill. When one side is brown, turn and cook the other side.

Split rolls in half and spread with butter.

Put rolls on plates. Spoon baked beans on rolls.

Sprinkle with cheese.

Put hot frankfurt on top of cheese. (Use tongs.)

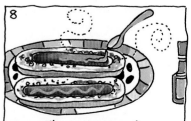

Top with a spoon of mustard and serve.

TASTY TUNA TRIANGLES

Makes 12 triangles

170 g can sandwich tuna
130 g can creamed corn
1 tablespoon chopped
    parsley leaves
1 egg
6 slices white bread
⅓ cup oil

1. Pour tuna and corn into a mixing bowl.

2. Add the chopped parsely and egg. Mix well.

3. Cut crusts off bread.

4. Spread mixture on bread slices.

5. Cut slices into triangles.

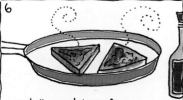

6. Heat the oil in a fry pan. When it's hot, put in a few triangles.

7. When they are golden lift out with a spatula and put on paper to drain.

8. Cook the rest of the triangles and drain on paper.

NACHOS

Serves 2

½ cup three bean mix
1 cup corn chips
¼ cup taco sauce
¼ cup chopped avocado
¼ cup grated mozzarella
   cheese
1 tablespoon sour cream

1 Turn oven to 180°c (350°F).

2  Put beans in a bowl. Mash with a fork.

3 Spoon beans into the centre of 2 ovenproof dishes.

4  Arrange corn chips around the beans.

5  Pour taco sauce on the beans.

6  Put avocado on top of sauce.

7  Sprinkle the grated cheese over.

8  Bake for 10 minutes. Serve topped with a spoonful of sour cream.

SAVOURY PUFF PINWHEELS

Makes about 12

1 sheet ready-rolled
  puff pastry
⅓ cup cream cheese
  spread
2 tablespoons tomato
  sauce

½ teaspoon dried oregano
  leaves
60 g sliced salami

Puff pastry is light flaky pastry made up of many thin layers. It is quite time-consuming to make, so we suggest you buy frozen puff pastry sheets from the supermarket.

1. Put the sheet of pastry on a big chopping board.

2. Spread the cheese spread over the pastry.

3. Spread the tomato sauce over.

4. Sprinkle with the oregano and the salami slices.

5. Roll up the pastry into a tight roll. Wrap in plastic wrap.

6. Put roll in the fridge for 1 hour.

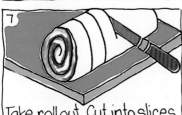

7. Take roll out. Cut into slices about 2cm wide. Turn oven to 200°c (400°F).

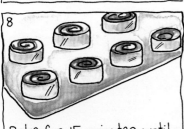

8. Bake for 15 minutes until crisp and golden.

SCHNITZEL SANDWICH

Makes 2

1/4 cup oil
1 onion, sliced
2 Vienna schnitzels
4 thick slices bread,
  lightly toasted
2 eggs
2 tablespoons barbecue
  sauce
1 tomato, sliced

1. Heat half the oil in a big, heavy fry pan.

2. Fry onions until brown. Take out of pan, drain on absorbent paper. Keep warm.

3. Pour the rest of the oil into the fry pan.

4. Cook schnitzels for 2 minutes. Turn over and cook the other side for 2 minutes.

5. Put schnitzels on toast. Top with onions.

6. Fry eggs. Put the cooked eggs on top of the onions.

7. Pour on sauce and put tomato on top.

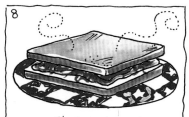

8. Top with toast and serve hot.

CHICKEN NOODLE OMELETTE

Serves 2

1 cup water
85 g packet chicken-
flavoured instant noodles
1 cup chopped cooked
chicken

2 teaspoons finely chopped
parsley
2 eggs, lightly beaten
2 tablespoons grated
Cheddar cheese

Omelettes are easy to make and good for you. You can add your favourite things; try chopped tomato and ham or salami. Bean sprouts and chopped celery give lots of crunch.

1
Boil the water in a small pan.

2
Add the noodles and flavour sachet to pan.

3
Cook noodles as directed. Drain well.

4
Put noodles, chicken, parsley and eggs in a bowl. Mix well.

5
Put the mixture in a 20cm non-stick fry pan.

6
Cook for 5 minutes without stirring.

7
Sprinkle with the cheese.

Put under a hot grill. Cook for 2 minutes to brown. Serve hot.

SUNKEN SUBMARINES

Makes 4

2 long crusty bread rolls
2 tablespoons garlic butter
225 g can spaghetti in
 tomato and cheese
 sauce
2 thick slices devon or ham
2 slices processed cheese

1. Heat oven to 180°C (350°F). Lightly grease an oven tray.

2. Cut rolls in half and spread with butter.

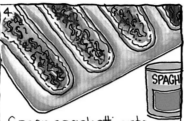

3. Put rolls on tray.

4. Spoon spaghetti onto each roll.

5. Chop devon and sprinkle over spaghetti.

6. Cut cheese into thin strips.

7. Arrange cheese strips on the devon.

8. Bake for 12 minutes. Serve hot.

CHICKEN POCKETS

Makes 2

2 oval pocket breads
2 tablespoons mayonnaise
3 large lettuce leaves
2 tablespoons corn relish
10 chicken nuggets

1 Carefully split pocket breads open.

2 Put bread on serving plates.

3 Spread mayonnaise on inside of bread.

4 Chop lettuce thinly.

5 Fill bread pockets with lettuce. Spoon relish over.

6 Grill chicken nuggets 3 minutes.

7 Turn nuggets; cook 3 minutes more.

8 Put cooked nuggets into pockets. Serve hot.

FRECKLE FACES

Makes about 12

1 cup self-raising flour
2 tablespoons caster sugar
1 egg, lightly beaten
½ cup milk
1 teaspoon imitation vanilla
  essence
1 teaspoon oil
¼ cup soft cream cheese
¼ cup hazelnut spread
2 tablespoons hundreds
  and thousands

1 Sift flour and sugar into a mixing bowl.

2 Add the egg, milk and vanilla. Beat with a fork until smooth.

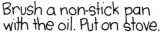

3 Brush a non-stick pan with the oil. Put on stove.

4 When pan is hot, put spoonfuls of mixture in about 4cm apart.

5 Cook for 1 minute, turn, cook other side for 1 minute or until bottom is golden.

6 Leave to cool. Spread half of each pikelet with cheese.

7 Spread other half with hazelnut spread.

Pancake batter can be made one day before you need it. Store in a jug, covered with plastic wrap, in the refrigerator.

8 Sprinkle with hundreds and thousands.

22

HAM AND CHEESE PUFFS

Makes 2
- 1 sheet ready-rolled puff pastry
- 1 teaspoon Vegemite
- 2 slices sandwich ham, cut in half
- 2 slices processed cheese
- 2 teaspoons fruit chutney

Turn oven to 180°c (350°F).

Put pastry on large cutting board. Cut into 4 squares.

Spread Vegemite over centre of 2 pieces.

Top with a slice of ham and cheese.

Spread cheese with chutney. Top with the rest of the ham.

Put the plain pastry on top. Press edges together.

Trim around edges with a pastry wheel.

Put on baking tray. Bake for 12 minutes.

23

CHOCANANA MUFFINS

Makes 12

1 small ripe banana
1 cup white self-raising
  flour
½ cup wholemeal
  self-raising flour
⅔ cup sugar
½ cup choc bits
1 egg, lightly beaten
⅔ cup milk
¼ cup oil

1. Turn oven to 180c (350°F).

2. Brush a 12-hole muffin pan with a little oil.

3. Mash banana in a large bowl.

4. Sift flour into the bowl (add the husks left in the sifter).

5. Put in sugar, choc bits, egg, milk and oil.

6. Stir with a fork until well mixed.

7. Spoon mixture into muffin pan. Fill the holes ⅔ full.

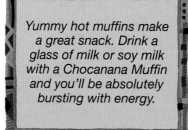

Yummy hot muffins make a great snack. Drink a glass of milk or soy milk with a Chocanana Muffin and you'll be absolutely bursting with energy.

8. Bake for 20 minutes or until golden. Turn onto a rack to cool.

FRUITY YOGHURT POPS

Makes 6

2 x 200 g cartons vanilla-
  flavoured yoghurt
170 g can passionfruit pulp
  in syrup
4 large strawberries
1 tablespoon icing sugar
ice choc magic or
  2 tablespoons melted
  chocolate

1. Put yoghurt and passionfruit in a mixing bowl.

2. Pull off green stems from strawberries.

3. Chop strawberries into small pieces. Put into bowl.

4. Add icing sugar to bowl. Mix well.

5. Spoon mixture into 6 ice-cream moulds or paper cups.

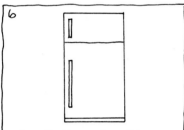

6. Put in freezer for 1 hour.

7. Press a wooden ice-cream stick in centre of each pop. Put back in freezer for 2 hours.

8. Turn pops out of mould or pull paper away. Drizzle with chocolate before eating.

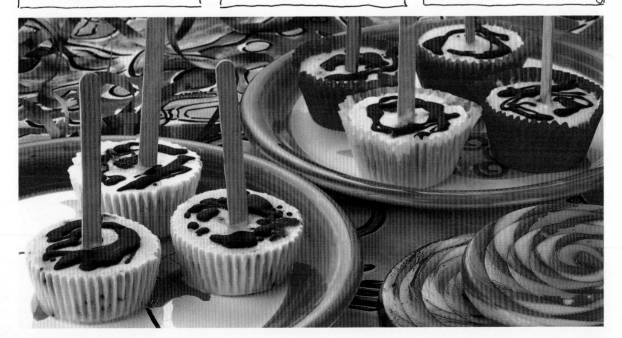

CHAPTER TWO

Two of Italy's special gifts to the world – pasta and pizza. Everybody loves them and they are so simple to make. To whip up a satisfying and scrumptious meal, simply choose your favourite recipe and add a crispy salad and a crunchy loaf of bread. Mmmm!

FABULOUS FETTUCCINE

Serves 4

375 g fettuccine
4 rashers bacon
220 g can mushrooms
   in butter sauce
130 g can creamed corn
2 medium zucchini
½ cup cream
3 spring onions, chopped
⅓ cup grated Parmesan
   cheese

1. Boil a big pot of water. Carefully add fettuccine.

2. Boil for 10 minutes. Drain well.

3. Chop bacon; throw away rinds. Fry gently.

4. Stir in mushrooms and corn.

5. Slice zucchini into rounds.

6. Add to pan with cream. Simmer for 5 minutes.

7. Add spring onions and Parmesan cheese. Stir.

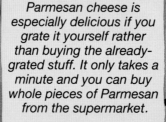

Parmesan cheese is especially delicious if you grate it yourself rather than buying the already-grated stuff. It only takes a minute and you can buy whole pieces of Parmesan from the supermarket.

8. Add pasta to pan and mix well. Serve immediately.

SPAGHETTI BOLOGNESE

Serves 4

2 tablespoons olive oil
1 medium onion, finely
    chopped
500 g minced beef
500 ml bottled spaghetti
    sauce
2 tablespoons tomato
    paste
¼ cup red wine
2 beef stock cubes,
    crumbled
½ cup frozen peas, rinsed
    and drained
2 cloves garlic, crushed
1 tablespoon finely
    chopped parsley
500 g packet spaghetti

¹ Heat oil in a big heavy pan.	² Fry onions and mince. Stir until all red has gone.	³ Add sauce, tomato paste, wine and stock cubes. Bring to boil.

4 Add peas. Turn down heat and simmer for 10 minutes.

5 Stir in garlic and parsley

6 Boil a big pot of water. Carefully add spaghetti.

7 Boil spaghetti for 10 minutes. Drain well.

Always cook spaghetti in a large pot of boiling water. The water is boiling when bubbles rise up to the surface and steam rises out of the pot.

8 Put spaghetti in a big serving bowl. Pour sauce over and serve.

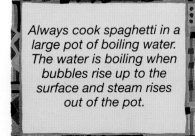

TUNA AND MACARONI BAKE

Serves 4

250 g macaroni
150 g corn kernels, drained
1 cup frozen peas, rinsed
  and drained
180 g can tuna in brine,
  drained

1 cup milk
22 g packet white
  sauce mix
½ cup sour cream
½ cup crushed cheese-
  flavoured biscuits

Tuna is a large, fast-swimming sea fish. They can weigh up to 750 kg each and live in warm ocean waters.

1. Turn oven to 180°c (350°F).

2. Boil a big pot of water. Carefully add macaroni.

3. Boil macaroni for 10 minutes. Drain well.

4. Put macaroni, corn, peas and tuna in a big bowl.

5. Put milk and sauce mix in a small pan. Stir until it boils and thickens.

6. Pour sauce into the bowl. Add cream. Mix well.

7. Put in a shallow casserole. Sprinkle with biscuits.

8. Bake for 20 minutes, then serve.

CORNY CHICKEN CANNELLONI

Serves 4

250 g packet frozen
   chopped leaf spinach
1 small onion, finely chopped
30 g butter
250 g chicken mince
130 g can corn kernels,
   drained
130 g can diced capsicum,
   drained
2 tablespoons dried
   breadcrumbs
1 egg, lightly beaten
120 g packet instant
   cannelloni shells
250 ml bottled spaghetti
   sauce
140 g jar cream cheese
   spread

1. Gently cook spinach, onion and butter in a small pan for 10 minutes.

2. Pour into a bowl and leave to cool.

3. Put mince into pan and cook, stirring, for 3 minutes.

4. Mix into spinach with corn, capsicum, breadcrumbs and egg.

5. Turn oven to 180°c (350°F). Spoon mixture into shells.

6. Spread 1/4 cup spaghetti sauce in a shallow casserole dish.

7. Arrange shells in dish. Pour remaining sauce over and dot with cheese.

8. Bake for 40 minutes. Take out, leave 5 minutes, then serve.

Pasta is made from durum flour, a special type of "hard" flour, mixed with eggs and rolled out to make spaghetti, shells, spirals, tubes, tiny stars, cartwheels and many other shapes.

MACARONI CHEESE

Serves 4

30 g butter
4 rashers bacon, cut
  in thin strips
2 tablespoons plain flour
2 cups milk
4 cups cooked macaroni

1 zucchini, finely chopped
1½ cups grated Cheddar
  cheese
1 tablespoon packaged
  breadcrumbs

1. Melt butter in a pan. Add bacon strips and cook 5 minutes.

2. Add flour and stir for 3 minutes.

3. Add milk a little at a time. Keep stirring.

4. Stir until sauce boils and is thick. Take pan off heat.

5. Add macaroni, zucchini and 1 cup cheese. Mix well.

6. Turn oven to 180°c (350°F). Spoon into a shallow ovenproof dish.

7. Sprinkle with the cheese and breadcrumbs.

Bake 25 minutes or until golden. Serve hot.

33

COMBINATION NOODLES

Serves 4

85 g sachet prawn-
flavoured noodles
1 cup water
2 tablespoons oil
100 g button mushrooms,
thinly sliced
4 rashers bacon, chopped
½ medium red capsicum
1 small carrot, coarsely
grated
130 g can corn kernels,
drained
3 spring onions, chopped
½ cup bean sprouts
2 teaspoons dark soy
sauce
1 tablespoon tomato sauce

1 Cook noodles, flavour sachet and water in a small pan.

2 Stir until liquid is absorbed. Cover and put to one side.

3 Heat oil in a big pan or wok.

4 Add chopped mushrooms and bacon, stir 5 minutes.

5 Cut capsicum in thin strips (throw away seeds). Add to pan.

6 Add carrot, corn, spring onions and bean sprouts. Stir well.

7 Add the cooked noodles, soy and tomato sauce. Stir well.

8 Cook for 2 minutes until hot, stirring gently. Serve immediately.

Italians aren't the only ones who love pasta. Asian-style cooking uses noodles (yes, they are pasta too!) in soups and stir-fried with meat and vegetables.

MEATY PIZZA WEDGES

Serves 4

375 g minced beef
¼ cup dried breadcrumbs
1 teaspoon dried oregano
   leaves
1 small onion, grated
½ medium red capsicum
60 g salami
3 tablespoons tomato
   purée
1 large tomato, sliced
½ cup grated mozzarella
   cheese

1

Turn oven to 200°C (400°F).

2

Put mince, breadcrumbs, oregano and onion in a big bowl.

3

Chop capsicum and salami finely. Add to bowl.

4

Add tomato purée and a little salt and pepper.

5

Use hands to knead mixture together.

6
Grease a deep 23cm pie dish. Press mixture into dish.

7

Arrange tomato over pizza. Sprinkle with cheese.

8

Bake 20 minutes. Pour off any liquid, slice and serve!

A short history of pizza, part 1. Long ago, the first simple pizzas were sold at street stalls in Naples, Italy. The sellers would sing songs in praise of their pizzas.

MEXICAN PITTA

Makes 3

3 pitta breads
½ cup refried beans
½ cup taco sauce
½ cup grated mozzarella
  cheese
½ medium green capsicum
9 black olives
9 corn chips
¼ cup sour cream

1. Turn oven to 200°c (400°F).

2. Grease a baking tray. Put pitta breads on tray.

3. Spread bread with beans. Top with taco sauce.

4. Chop capsicum finely (throw away seeds).

5. Sprinkle capsicum and grated cheese over sauce.

6. Arrange olives and chips on top.

7. Bake for 15 minutes.

8. Put a spoonful of sour cream in centre just before serving.

PINEAPPLE PAN PIZZA

Serves 2

2 teaspoons oil
1 Lebanese bread
2 tablespoons tomato paste
½ teaspoon dried oregano leaves

100 g Cheddar cheese
125 g sliced ham
60 g pepperoni
2 canned pineapple rings, drained

A short history of pizza, part 2. From humble beginnings, pizza has become one of the most popular foods ever. Pizza is eaten in nearly every country in the world.

1. Grease a big non-stick pan with the oil.

2. Spread bread with tomato paste. Sprinkle on oregano.

3. Grate cheese coarsely. Sprinkle over bread.

4. Put bread in pan.

5. Cut ham and pepperoni into thin strips.

6. Arrange over bread.

7. Chop pineapple rings and arrange over pizza.

8. Cover pizza and cook gently for 8 minutes.

PIZZA SUPREME

Serves 4

1 large frozen pizza base
½ cup bottled spaghetti sauce
2 cups grated mozzarella cheese
1 onion
125 g button mushrooms
½ medium green capsicum
200 g can peeled prawns, drained
100 g cabanossi
100 g pepperoni
12 black olives, pitted

1. Turn oven to 200°C (400°F).

2. Grease pizza tray. Put pizza base on tray.

3. Spread with spaghetti sauce and ½ the cheese.

4. Cut onion, mushrooms and capsicum (throw away seeds) into thin slices.

5. Arrange vegetables on pizza.

6. Sprinkle prawns and remaining cheese over.

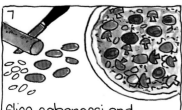

7. Slice cabanossi and pepperoni. Arrange on pizza with olives.

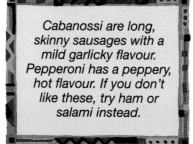

Cabanossi are long, skinny sausages with a mild garlicky flavour. Pepperoni has a peppery, hot flavour. If you don't like these, try ham or salami instead.

Bake 25 minutes. Serve hot.

MINCE 'N' MUSHROOM PIZZA

Serves 4

2 tablespoons oil
340 g packet scone mix
⅓ cup grated Cheddar
  cheese
125 g minced beef
200 g button mushrooms,
  thinly sliced
1 cup tomato purée
1 teaspoon dried mixed
  herbs
1 clove garlic, crushed
6 cherry tomatoes,
  cut in half
6 slices processed cheese,
  cut into thin strips
6 black olives

1
Turn oven to 200°c (400°F).

2
Brush a 30cm × 20cm shallow pan with 1 tablespoon oil.

3
Follow directions on packet to make scone dough.

4
Knead cheese into dough. Press dough into tin.

5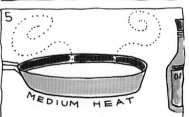
MEDIUM HEAT
Heat remaining oil in pan and cook mince until all red is gone

6
LOW HEAT
Add mushrooms, tomato purée, mixed herbs and garlic. Simmer 10 minutes.

7
Pour over scone base. Decorate with tomatoes, cheese and olives.

To peel garlic, cut garlic clove longways, then you can easily pull off the skin. To crush, cover with the wide, flat blade of a knife; hit the knife with your hand.

8
Bake 25 minutes. Serve hot.

CHAPTER THREE

CHICKEN, MEAT AND SEAFOOD

These are substantial, main meal dishes that will really impress when you serve them up. The burgers are a meal on their own, but you might like to serve your favourite vegetables and a baked potato (see page 74) with the other recipes. Add a luscious dessert from Chapter 5 and you'll be sure to have a great success on your hands.

CHICKEN FILLET BURGERS

Makes 2

1 egg, lightly beaten
¼ cup cornflour
1 cup cornflake crumbs
2 tablespoons desiccated
  coconut
2 chicken breast fillets
2 tablespoons oil
2 hamburger buns

1 banana, sliced diagonally
½ cup shredded lettuce
½ cup grated carrot
¼ cup alfalfa sprouts
¼ cup fruit chutney
⅓ cup grated Cheddar
  cheese

Burgers can be a really healthy, energy-giving meal – use lean minced meat, chicken or fish, be generous with the salad ingredients and use wholemeal buns.

1 Put egg and cornflour in a small bowl. Mix until smooth.

2 Put cornflake crumbs and coconut on a flat plate.

3 Dip chicken into egg mixture and then roll in crumbs.

4 Heat oil in a big, heavy pan.

5 Add chicken and cook 3 minutes. Turn and cook other side 3 minutes until golden.

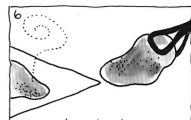
6 Take out and put on paper towels to drain.

7 Open up buns. Put banana, lettuce, carrot and alfalfa on bottom halves.

8 Add chicken, chutney and grated cheese. Put top on. Serve immediately.

CHINESE LEMON CHICKEN

Serves 4

12 chicken wings
1 stick celery
1 small carrot
1 medium red capsicum
3 teaspoons cornflour
2 teaspoons brown sugar
¼ teaspoon ground ginger
⅓ cup lemon juice
1 cup rich chicken stock

1. Wash chicken wings and pat dry.

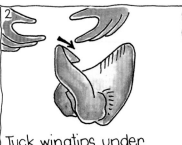

2. Tuck wingtips under.

3. Put cornflour, sugar, ginger and lemon juice in a pan. Mix until smooth.

4. Cut celery, carrot and capsicum (throw away seeds) into long thin strips.

5. Add to cornflour mixture. Pour in chicken stock.

6. MEDIUM HEAT
Stir until sauce boils and thickens.

7. MEDIUM HEAT
Grill chicken for 8 minutes; turn and cook other side 8 minutes until golden.

8. Put chicken on a serving plate. Pour sauce over. Serve hot with rice.

FRIED RICE

Serves 4

⅓ cup oil
1 cup long-grain rice
1½ cups chicken stock
½ cup frozen peas, rinsed
  and drained
½ medium red capsicum,
  finely chopped
100 g button mushrooms,
  thinly sliced
2 eggs, lightly beaten
2 spring onions, chopped
200 g can peeled prawns
300 g cooked Chinese
  barbecued pork,
  cut into thin strips
1 tablespoon soy sauce
2 teaspoons sesame oil

1
Heat 2 tablespoons oil in a pan. Add rice. Stir 5 minutes or until golden.

2
Pour in stock. Turn down heat, put lid on. Simmer 15 minutes or until rice is tender.

3
Add peas. Cover and put to one side.

4
Heat 1 tablespoon oil in wok. Add capsicum. Stir 1 minute. Drain on paper towels.

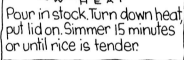

5
Add rest of oil. Add mushrooms. Stir 1 minute. Drain with capsicum.

6
Add eggs. Swirl over base — don't stir.

7
When cooked like an omelette, lift out and slice.

When heating oil, smoke means the oil is too hot and will burn food. Turn down heat and gently take the pan off the heat for a few minutes before adding food.

8
Put all ingredients into wok. Add soy sauce and sesame oil. Stir until hot.

CHICKEN SATAYS

Makes 12

6 chicken thighs, skinned, boned
2 teaspoons soy sauce
⅓ cup crunchy peanut butter
2 tablespoons lemon juice
150 g can coconut cream
1 tablespoon sweet chilli sauce
¼ teaspoon garam masala

1
Cut chicken in long, thin strips.

2
Put chicken and soy sauce in a bowl. Stir to cover chicken with sauce.

3
In another bowl, mix peanut butter and lemon juice together.

4
Add coconut cream, chilli sauce and garam masala. Mix well.

5
Mix 2 tablespoons peanut sauce into chicken.

6
Thread chicken onto skewers.

7
Grill for 3 minutes. Turn chicken and grill other side for 3 minutes.

Buy packets of bamboo or metal skewers from the supermarket. Soak the bamboo skewers in water to prevent them burning under the hot grill. Use gloves to pick up hot skewers.

8
Put peanut sauce in a small pan. Cook 5 minutes until hot. Spoon over chicken and serve.

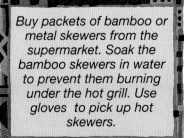

CRISPY CHICKEN ROLLS

Makes 4

⅓ cup mango chutney
1 tablespoon sour cream
2 spring onions, finely
   chopped
8 sheets filo pastry
4 chicken breast fillets,
   skinless
60 g butter, melted

1
Turn oven to 180°c (350°F).
Lightly grease an oven tray.

2

Put chutney, cream and spring onions in a small bowl. Mix well.

3

Lay out one sheet of filo pastry. Put another sheet on top. Fold in ½ longways.

4

Put a chicken fillet at one end. Spoon ¼ mango mixture onto chicken.

5

Roll pastry once over chicken. Fold sides over and keep rolling to make a parcel.

6

Repeat to make 3 more chicken parcels.

7

Arrange parcels on tray and brush with melted butter.

8

Bake 20 minutes or until golden. Serve hot.

LAMB KEBABS

Serves 4

8 lamb chump chops
200 g carton plain yoghurt
2 cloves garlic, crushed
1 teaspoon ground turmeric
2 teaspoons tomato paste
¼ teaspoon ground ginger
¼ teaspoon garam masala

1. Trim bones and any fat from chops and throw away.

2. Cut meat into 2cm cubes.

3. Mix yoghurt, garlic, turmeric, tomato paste, ginger and garam masala in a bowl.

4. Add meat. Stir to cover meat with sauce.

5. Cover bowl with plastic wrap. Put in fridge for 2 hours.

6. Thread meat onto skewers.

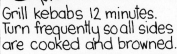

7. MEDIUM HEAT
Grill kebabs 12 minutes. Turn frequently so all sides are cooked and browned.

8. Serve hot with a salad.

SAUSAGE AND BEAN BAKE

Serves 4

1 large onion
3 slices bacon,
2 sticks celery, sliced
4 continental sausages,
   sliced
2 spring onions, finely
   chopped

1 tablespoon finely
   chopped parsley
225 g can baked beans in
   tomato sauce
1 tablespoon tomato paste
½ cup water

Serve this dish with a crispy green salad and hot bread rolls. Put rolls on an oven tray; place in the oven for the last 15 minutes of cooking time.

1. Turn oven to 180°c (350°F).

2. Chop onion and bacon finely. (Throw away bacon rind.)

3. Mix onion, bacon, celery and sausage in a big bowl.

4. Add spring onions and parsley. Mix well.

5. Stir in baked beans, tomato paste and water.

6. Spread mixture into a shallow ovenproof dish.

7. Put lid on or cover with foil. Bake 20 minutes.

8. Take off lid or foil and bake for 15 minutes more. Serve hot.

LAMB HOT POT

Serves 4

1 large onion
2 large carrots
250 g button mushrooms
2 large potatoes
410 g can tomatoes,
  crushed

8 lamb chump chops
¼ cup lemon juice
½ teaspoon dried oregano
  leaves
1 tablespoon chicken stock
  powder

This dish takes a while to cook, so add up the cooking times mentioned (45 + 20 mins = 1 hr 5 mins) and begin cooking 1 hour 5 minutes before you want to eat.

1 Turn oven to 180°c (350°F).

2 Chop onion and carrots. Cut mushrooms in half.

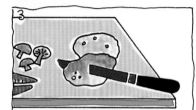
3 Cut each potato into 8 pieces.

4 Trim fat from chops and throw away.

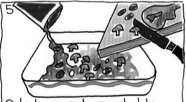
5 Put chopped vegetables, canned tomatoes and chops into a casserole dish.

6 Put lemon juice, oregano and stock powder in a jug. Mix well. Pour over meat and vegetables.

7 Put lid on or cover with foil. Bake 45 minutes.

8 Remove lid or foil, stir the casserole, and bake for 20 minutes more. Serve hot.

49

LAMB AND APRICOT PARCELS

Makes 6

100 g dried apricots, finely
  chopped
500 g minced lamb
½ cup apricot conserve
½ cup herb stuffing mix
3 sheets ready-rolled puff
  pastry
1 egg, lightly beaten

1
Turn oven to 180°c (350°F).

2
Mix apricots, lamb, conserve
and stuffing mix. Leave
20 minutes.

3
Shape mince into 6 flat,
square patties, about
10cm × 10cm.

4
Cut pastry sheets in ½ to
make 6 pieces. Put a pattie
on the end of each piece.

5
Brush pastry with
beaten egg.

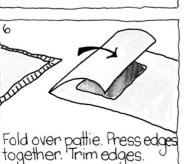

6
Fold over pattie. Press edges
together. Trim edges.

7
Cut 3 slits in top of each
parcel with a sharp knife.

8
Brush with egg. Bake for
30 minutes until crisp
and golden.

CRISPY TEX-MEX CASSEROLE

Serves 6

1 tablespoon oil
500 g minced beef
410 g can tomatoes,
   crushed
425 g can red kidney beans
¼ teaspoon cumin
500 g potatoes, thinly sliced
1 cup grated Cheddar
   cheese
50 g packet corn chips

1 Heat oil in a big, heavy pan. Fry mince 5 minutes.

2 Add tomatoes, kidney beans and cumin. Stir.

3 Turn down heat and simmer 15 minutes, stirring every now and then.

4 Turn oven to 180°C (350°F). In a bowl mix potatoes with cheese.

5 Layer ⅓ of the potatoes on base of an ovenproof dish. Spoon ½ the mince on top.

6 Top with another potato layer, another mince layer and finish with potatoes.

7 Bake for 45 minutes.

8 Spread corn chips over top. Bake for 15 minutes more. Serve hot.

"Tex-Mex" means a dish with the typical flavours of Texas and Mexico, usually beans, beef, corn, cheese, cumin (a herb) and sometimes chilli.

51

HEARTY BEEF PIE

Serves 4

500 g rump steak
2 tablespoons oil
500 g button mushrooms,
   cut in half
2 onions, sliced
2 tablespoons plain flour
1 teaspoon mixed dried
   herbs
2 cups water
3 beef stock cubes,
   crumbled
2 teaspoons
   Worcestershire sauce
285 g packet flaky
   pastry mix

1

Turn oven to 180°C (350°F).

2

Cut steak into 2 cm cubes. Trim any fat off and throw away.

3

Heat oil in a deep, heavy pan. Add steak and cook, stirring for 5 minutes.

4

MEDIUM HEAT

Add mushrooms and onions. Stir 10 minutes until well browned.

5

MEDIUM HEAT

Stir in flour and herbs. Add water, stock cubes and sauce. Stir.

6

LOW HEAT

Put lid on and simmer 15 minutes. Pour into a deep 23 cm pie dish.

7

Follow directions on packet to make pastry dough. Roll out to fit pie dish.

Don't peel or wash mushrooms before you use them, as this takes away flavour. Just wipe them with a damp cloth to remove any earth, then use as directed.

8

Cover dish with pastry. Make a few holes with a fork. Bake for 20 minutes.

HAMBURGER WITH THE LOT

Makes 4

500 g hamburger mince
110 g packet hamburger
   seasoning mix
¼ cup oil
1 large onion,
   sliced into rings
4 rashers bacon
4 eggs

4 hamburger buns
4 slices Cheddar cheese
1 cup shredded lettuce
1 medium tomato, sliced
8 slices beetroot, well
   drained
4 pineapple rings
⅓ cup tomato sauce

Wash lettuce well to get rid of dirt and any bugs that may be hiding among the leaves. Wash under running water and then dry with paper towels.

1. Mix mince and seasoning in a bowl. Shape into 4 patties.

2. Heat oil in a big, heavy pan. Fry patties 3 minutes, turn and cook other side 3 minutes.

3. Drain on paper towels, cover and keep warm.

4. Fry onions until golden; drain on paper towels.

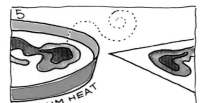

5. Fry bacon until crisp; drain on paper towels.

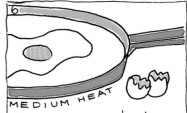

6. Fry eggs one at a time; keep warm.

7. Cut open buns. Toast until golden.

8. Lay everything on bun bottoms. Top with sauce, put top on and serve.

SPARERIBS IN PLUM SAUCE

Serves 6

1 kg rack American-style
    pork spareribs
⅓ cup plum jam
1 tablespoon dark
    soy sauce
1 tablespoon Thai sweet
    chilli sauce
¼ teaspoon Chinese
    five-spice powder
3 teaspoons cornflour
½ cup chicken stock

1

Turn oven to 200°c (400°F).

2

Put ribs onto a rack in a shallow baking dish.

3

Bake for 25 minutes. Turn ribs once during cooking.

4.

Heat jam, soy and chilli sauce and five-spice powder in a small pan.

5

Mix cornflour and chicken stock together until smooth.

6

Pour into pan. Stir gently until plum sauce boils and thickens.

7

When ribs are cooked, pull ribs apart. Arrange on a serving dish.

American-style spareribs are thinner and less fatty than pork spareribs. If you use pork spareribs for this recipe, trim most of the fat away before you cook them.

8
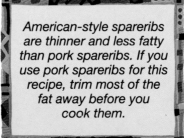
Pour plum sauce over. Serve immediately.

ASIAN BEEF AND VEGETABLES

Serves 6

750 g rump steak
2 spring onions, chopped
2 cloves garlic, crushed
2 tablespoons barbecue
   sauce
¼ cup oyster sauce
¼ teaspoon ground ginger
2 tablespoons oil
1 large onion, sliced
3 cups finely sliced
   vegetables (celery,
   broccoli, baby corn,
   carrot)

1. Trim any fat and throw it away. Cut beef into long, thin strips.

2. Put beef in a bowl. Add spring onions, garlic, barbecue and oyster sauces and ginger. Mix.

3. Heat oil in wok. Divide meat into 3 lots.

4. Add one lot of meat, stir quickly for 30 seconds.

5. Lift meat onto a plate. Repeat until all meat is cooked.

6. Add onion to wok. Stir for 2 minutes.

7. Add chopped vegetables. Stir for 3 minutes.

Stir-frying food seals in the goodness. To stir-fry, quickly move vegies or meat around the wok with a large spoon or spatula. Don't let them sit in the bottom as they will burn.

8. Add meat to wok. Stir for 5 minutes. Serve immediately with rice.

FANCY FISH FINGERS

Serves 4

1/3 cup tomato relish
12 fish fingers
3 slices processed cheese
4 rashers bacon

Turn oven to 200°c (400°F).

Spread relish on one side of each fish finger.

Cut each cheese slice into 4 strips.

Lay a slice over relish.

Cut bacon into long thin strips.

Wrap bacon around each finger.

Place fingers on an oven tray (you don't need to grease the tray).

Bake 10 minutes. Serve hot.

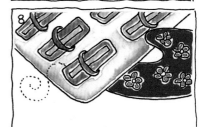

SALMON PASTA POTS

Serves 3

1 cup small spiral pasta
210 g can pink salmon
1 small carrot
1 spring onion, finely
  chopped
¼ cup mayonnaise

⅓ cup cream
½ red capsicum,
  finely chopped
2 tablespoons chopped
  parsley

Tinned salmon is very high in calcium, especially if you eat the bones (they are quite soft and safe to eat). Calcium gives us strong bones and teeth.

1 Boil a big pot of water. Carefully add spiral pasta.

2 Boil for 10 minutes. Drain well.

3 Turn oven to 180°c (350°F).

4 Tip salmon into a mixing bowl. Mash with a fork.

5 Grate carrot over salmon. Add spring onion.

6 Add pasta, mayonnaise, cream, capsicum and parsley to bowl.

7 Spoon mixture into 3 small ovenproof pots.

Bake for 15 minutes or until heated through. Serve hot.

CHAPTER FOUR

MICROWAVE

The microwave oven makes cooking simple and convenient. The yummy recipes in this chapter cover soup, main meal dishes, puddings and cakes. Don't forget to read the special microwave cooking instructions at the front of the book before you start.

SPICY LAMB CURRY

Serves 4

2 tablespoons oil
1 large onion, thinly sliced
2 teaspoons curry powder
¼ teaspoon garam masala
½ teaspoon dried coriander
    leaves
1 medium apple, chopped
750 g lamb chump chops,
    boned, cut into 3 cm
    pieces
1 large carrot, chopped
150 g can coconut cream
½ cup rich chicken stock
12 pappadums

1

Put oil and onion in a deep dish. Cook on High for 2 minutes.

2

Add curry powder, garam masala and coriander. Cook on High for 1 minute.

3

Add apple, lamb and carrot. Mix gently.

4
Stir in coconut cream and stock.

5

Cover and cook on Medium/High for 25 minutes. Stir halfway through cooking.

6

Leave 10 minutes before serving.

7

Put 2 pappadums in microwave. Cook on High until they puff up.

Pappadums are like large chips – light, crispy and delicious. They are made from lentil flour and they "grow" as they cook. Buy them from the supermarket.

8

Repeat until all pappadums are cooked. Serve with curry and rice.

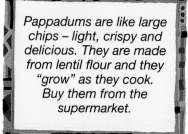

EASY APRICOT CHICKEN

Serves 4

1 tablespoon flour
40 g sachet French onion
   soup mix
8 chicken drumsticks
   (about 1 kg)
2 medium zucchini,
   chopped
1 large onion, coarsely
   grated
½ teaspoon grated lemon
   rind
¾ cup apricot nectar
425 g can apricot halves,
   drained

1. Put flour and soup mix in a plastic bag.

2. Add chicken. Hold top firmly and shake until well coated.

3. Put chicken in a shallow dish.

4. Top with zucchini.

5. Stir onion, lemon rind and apricot nectar together.

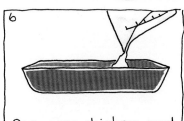

6. Pour over chicken and zucchini.

7. Arrange apricots on top.

To grate lemon rind, use the side of the grater with the smallest holes. Hold over a plate and gently rub lemon skin. Don't press too hard or you'll get the bitter white pith.

8. Cover and cook on Medium/High for 30 minutes. Stir once during cooking.

PEA AND HAM SOUP

Serves 4

375 g smoked bacon
  pieces
2 large potatoes, chopped
1 L water
1 cup frozen peas
3 teaspoons lemon juice
crusty bread

1

Put bacon, potatoes and water in a deep dish.

2

Cover and cook on High for 20 minutes.

3

Take out bacon. Chop the meat. Throw away the bones.

4

Mash the potatoes until smooth.

5

Put bacon pieces back into the dish.

6

Add peas and potatoes.

7

Cover and cook on High for 5 minutes.

8

Stir in lemon juice. Serve with crusty bread.

SAVOURY RICE RING

Serves 4-6

3 rashers bacon
1½ cups cooked long-grain rice
190 g can mushrooms, drained and thinly sliced
1 medium zucchini, coarsely grated
1 large carrot, coarsely grated
4 eggs, lightly beaten
1½ cups grated Cheddar cheese

1. Grease a deep, 25cm glass ring dish.

2. Chop bacon into small pieces, throw away rind.

3. Put bacon, rice and vegetables in a bowl. Mix well.

4. Pour eggs over.

5. Add grated cheese. Mix well.

6. Press mixture into ring.

7. Cover and cook on Medium High for 12 minutes.

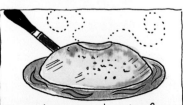

8. Stand 5 minutes before serving. Turn out and cut into slices.

To cook rice: place ¾ cup of raw rice into a large pan of boiling water. Cook for 12-15 minutes; pour into a colander to drain. This makes 1½ cups of cooked rice.

MINI MINCE CUPS

Makes 6

285 g can mushrooms,
   drained and sliced
1 kg pork and veal mince
2 tablespoons bacon-
   flavoured chips, crushed
⅓ cup tomato chilli pickle
1 cup dried breadcrumbs

1 tablespoon finely
   chopped parsley
1 teaspoon dried oregano
   leaves
1 egg, lightly beaten
bottled sweet and sour
   sauce

Serve with a salad and microwaved jacket potatoes. See page 74 for how to cook potatoes in the microwave. Top cooked potatoes with a little butter.

1 Grease 6 microwave-safe cups with oil.

2 Put mushrooms on paper towels. Wrap paper around and squeeze gently to dry.

3 Put mushrooms, mince, chips, pickle, breadcrumbs, parsley and oregano in a big bowl.

4 Add egg. Knead with hands until smooth.

5 Cover with plastic wrap. Put in fridge for 1 hour.

6 Press mixture evenly into cups.

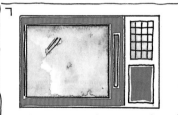

7 Cook on a rack on Medium/High for 10 minutes.

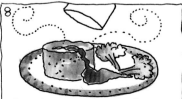

8 Stand 5 minutes before serving. Turn out and serve with sauce.

BEEF STROGANOFF

Serves 4

1 tablespoon oil
1 large onion, thinly sliced
200 g baby mushrooms,
   thinly sliced
½ cup water
1 chicken stock cube,
   crumbled
2 teaspoons tomato paste
1 teaspoon French mustard
1 tablespoon sour cream
500 g rump steak cut into
   thin flat strips
1 tablespoon plain flour
2 teaspoons paprika

1  Put oil, onion and mushrooms in a deep casserole dish.

2  Cover and cook on High for 3 minutes. Stir.

3  Take off lid, cook on High for 3 minutes. Stir.

4  Put water, stock cube, tomato paste, mustard and cream in a jug. Mix well.

5  Pour over onion and mushrooms. Stir.

6  Cover and cook on High for 3 minutes.

7  Mix flour, paprika and a little pepper on a flat plate. Coat meat with mixture.

8  Add meat to dish. Stir. Cover and cook on Medium for 10 minutes. Serve with rice.

When serving, add an extra dollop of sour cream and some chopped chives to make this dish extra-special.

CHEESY SAUSAGE SLICE

Serves 4

4 slices wholemeal bread,
  buttered one side
2 continental frankfurts
  or 1 stick cabanossi
1 small onion
1 small zucchini
1 tablespoon self-raising
  flour
2 teaspoons finely chopped
  parsley
2 eggs, lightly beaten
½ cup grated mozzarella
  cheese

1 Cut crusts off bread.

2 Arrange, butter side up, on bottom of a shallow, round 23cm dish.

3 Cut frankfurts or cabanossi into thin slices.

4 Coarsely grate onion and zucchini into a bowl.

5 Add frankfurts or cabanossi, flour and parsley. Mix well.

6 Add eggs and cheese. Stir well.

7 Spoon over bread. Cover with plastic wrap.

8 Cook on a rack on Medium High for 8 minutes. Serve hot or cold.

To save time, grate cheese beforehand. Hold grater over a plate and grate the amount needed. Cover with plastic wrap, store in refrigerator.

HAZELNUT FUDGE CAKE

Serves 6

60 g butter
125 g dark chocolate, chopped
2 tablespoons hazelnut spread
2 eggs, lightly beaten
2 tablespoons sugar
½ cup self-raising flour
⅓ cup chopped hazelnuts
½ cup hazelnut spread, extra

1

Lightly grease a 20cm round cake dish.

2

Put butter and chocolate in a medium bowl.

3

Cook on Medium for 1 minute. Stir until smooth.

4

Add hazelnut spread, eggs, sugar, flour and nuts. Mix well.

5

Spread evenly in cake dish.

6

Cook on a rack on Medium/High for 4 minutes.

7

Leave in dish for 10 minutes then turn out onto a serving plate.

8

Decorate top and sides with extra spread. Put in fridge for 20 minutes. Serve.

Decorate this cake with chocolate buttons, chocolate animals or whatever takes your fancy.

GOLDEN CARROT PUDDINGS

Makes 4

4 teaspoons golden syrup
1⅓ cups coarsely grated
  carrot
½ cup chopped pecan nuts
½ cup sugar
⅔ cup wholemeal self-
  raising flour

½ teaspoon mixed spice
¼ teaspoon ground
  cinnamon
⅓ cup oil
1 egg, lightly beaten
whipped cream, to serve

*Whip cream in a blender,
with electric beaters or
with a whisk. Have the
cream very cold
If you whip too long it will
turn to butter: stop when
it is just becoming thick
and stiff.*

1 Lightly grease 4 microwave safe cups with oil.

2 Put a teaspoon of syrup into each cup.

3 Put carrot, nuts and sugar in a bowl.

4 Sift flour, spice and cinnamon over.

5 Add egg and oil. Mix well.

6 Spoon evenly into cups. Smooth tops.

7 Cook on rack on Medium/ High 8 minutes.

8 Leave in dish 10 minutes. Turn out. Serve with whipped cream.

APRICOT-STUDDED PUDDING

Serves 4-6

½ cup finely chopped dried apricots

⅓ cup fresh orange juice

6 slices wholemeal bread, buttered one side

¼ cup sugar

1 tablespoon custard powder

3 eggs, lightly beaten

½ teaspoon finely grated orange rind

1½ cups milk

1 tablespoon brown sugar

cream or ice-cream

This lovely bread pudding is also delicious made with dates instead of apricots.

1 Put apricots and juice in a small bowl. Cover and cook on Medium 4 minutes.

2 Cut crusts off bread. Cut each slice into small squares.

3 Arrange on bottom of a shallow ovenproof dish.

4 Put sugar, custard powder, eggs and rind in a bowl. Stir.

5 Put milk into big jug. Cook on High for 2 minutes or until very hot.

6 Pour onto egg mixture. Whisk until smooth.

7 Pour gently over bread. Sprinkle with the apricots and brown sugar.

8 Cover. Cook on rack on High 4 minutes. Stand 5 minutes.

SPIKY CRACKLES

Makes 16 squares

250 g packet jersey
   caramels, chopped
1 tablespoon golden syrup
60 g butter
250 g dark chocolate, finely
   chopped
3 cups Rice Bubbles
100 g white marshmallows,
   chopped
⅓ cup toasted slivered
   almonds

1 Line base and sides of a 23cm square dish with foil. (Don't put this in the microwave!)

2 Put caramels, golden syrup, butter and ½ the chocolate in a bowl.

3 Cook (uncovered) on Medium for 2 minutes. Stir until smooth.

4 Mix Rice Bubbles into caramel. Press into dish.

5 Put chocolate and marshmallows in a bowl.

6 Cook on Medium 45 seconds. Beat until smooth.

7 Spread over caramel mixture. Press nuts on top.

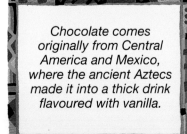

Chocolate comes originally from Central America and Mexico, where the ancient Aztecs made it into a thick drink flavoured with vanilla.

8 Leave to set, cut into fingers and serve.

CHOCOLATE FUDGE SAUCE

Makes 2 cups

125 g dark chocolate, finely
  chopped
400 g can sweetened
  condensed milk
100 g white marshmallows

1 Put chocolate and condensed milk in a medium bowl.

2 Cook on Medium for 1 minute. Stir.

3 Cut marshmallows into small pieces.

4 Stir into chocolate mixture.

5 Cook on Medium for 1 minute.

6 Beat until almost smooth.

7 Cook on Medium for 1 minute. Stir.

8 Serve hot or cold with ice-cream.

BUTTERSCOTCH BANANAS

60 g butter **Serves 4**
¼ cup brown sugar
¼ cup golden syrup
2 teaspoons lemon juice
2 tablespoons sour cream
3 bananas
2 tablespoons toasted
  flaked almonds
vanilla ice-cream

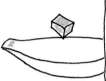

Put butter in a shallow, oblong dish. Cook on Medium for 45 seconds.

2
Add sugar and syrup. Stir until thick and smooth.

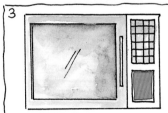

3
Cook on High for 2 minutes.

4
Add juice and cream. Stir well. Cook on High for 2 minutes.

5
Cut bananas in half longways and crossways.

6
Arrange in dish in 1 layer. Stir to coat with sauce.

7
Cook on Medium 4 minutes. Turn, cook 4 minutes more.

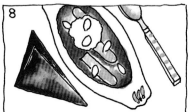

8
Sprinkle with almonds. Serve with ice-cream.

STICKY BUNS

Serves 6

340 g packet scone mix
1 tablespoon brown sugar
½ teaspoon ground
   cinnamon
½ - ⅔ cup water
30 g butter, melted
1 cup mixed dried fruit
8 glacé cherries
1 tablespoon brown sugar,
   extra
PINK ICING
¾ cup icing sugar, sifted
2 teaspoons milk
60 g butter, melted
2 drops pink food colouring

1

Sift scone mix, sugar and cinnamon into a bowl.

2

Add enough water to mix to a soft dough.

3
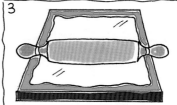
Turn out, knead gently, roll out to 30 × 35 cm.

4

Brush with butter, sprinkle with sugar and fruit.

5

Roll up, cut into 6 slices, arrange on round dish.

6

Cook on a rack on Medium/High 8 minutes.

7

Turn onto a wire rack to cool. Put cherries on top.

These buns are perfect for morning or afternoon tea. Make them as a surprise for mum or dad, with a cup of tea or coffee.

8

Mix sugar, milk, butter and colouring until smooth, drizzle over bun.

YUMMY BAKED POTATOES

Potatoes baked or microwaved in their skins or jackets are absolutely delicious. You can eat them hot or cold, just as they are or serve them with a dollop of sour cream or butter. Best of all, scoop out the middle and make one of our delicious recipes.

Baked potatoes are great on their own as a snack or served with a crunchy salad for a light meal. Serve one or two potatoes for each person. A baked potato in your school lunchbox will make a great change from sandwiches.

To make baked potatoes really crispy, brush the skin with a little oil and sprinkle with salt before cooking. To check if potatoes are cooked, hold potato firmly with an oven mitt or dry tea-towel. Push a skewer into the centre of the potato. If it goes in easily, the potato is cooked.

BEFORE YOU COOK

• Don't buy potatoes that look greenish.
• Old potatoes are best for baking.
• Choose potatoes that are about the same size and shape, so they will cook at the same time.
• Scrub potatoes under cold water. Pat dry with paper towels. Do not peel.

HOW TO BAKE POTATOES

Turn oven to 210°C (415°F). Pierce potatoes all over with a fork — this helps potato to cook evenly and to prevent the skin splitting. Place directly on the oven rack. Bake 1 hour or until tender. Remove from oven and cool slightly. Cut potatoes in half with a sharp knife. Scoop out the flesh with a teaspoon, leaving a thin shell. Try not to put a hole in the shell. Use the scooped out potato in the filling.

HOW TO MICROWAVE POTATOES

Pierce potatoes all over with a fork. Wrap each one in a layer of absorbent paper and place directly onto the turntable. For four potatoes, cook on High for 10 minutes. Leave, unopened, for 2 minutes before cutting. Scoop out the flesh with a teaspoon, leaving a thin shell. Try not to put a hole in the shell. Use the scooped out potato in the filling.

Scrub potatoes well. Pierce potatoes all over with a fork.

Place potato directly on oven rack. Bake for 1 hour.

To microwave, pierce potatoes and wrap in absorbent paper. Cook on High.

BOLOGNESE POTATOES

4 medium potatoes
1 tablespoon oil
125 g minced beef
1 tablespoon tomato paste
¼ cup water
130 g can spaghetti with
  cheese and tomato sauce
1 spring onion, chopped
2 tablespoons grated
  Parmesan cheese

1 Turn oven to 210°C (415°F).
  Pierce potatoes. Place on
  oven rack. Bake 1 hour OR
  microwave on High for 10
  minutes.
2 Cut potatoes in half, scoop
  out flesh. Arrange potato
  shells on oven tray.
3 Heat oil in a small pan. Add
  mince. Cook 3 minutes until
  brown. Add tomato paste
  and water. Stir and bring to
  the boil.
4 Remove from heat. Stir in
  spaghetti, onion and cheese.
5 Mash scooped out flesh in a
  bowl. Mix gently into
  spaghetti mixture. Spoon filling into shells.
6 Bake 15 minutes OR
  microwave on Medium for
  5 minutes. Serve hot.

CRUNCHY TUNA POTATOES

4 medium potatoes
185 g can tuna in oil, drained
¼ cup mayonnaise
1 stick celery, finely chopped
2 tablespoons finely chopped
  red capsicum
1 tablespoon finely chopped
  parsley
½ cup breadcrumbs

1 Turn oven to 210°C (415°F).
  Pierce potatoes. Place on
  oven rack. Bake 1 hour OR
  microwave on High for 10
  minutes.
2 Cut potatoes in half, scoop
  out flesh. Arrange potato
  shells on oven tray.
3 Mash scooped-out potato in
  a bowl. Add tuna, mayonnaise, celery, capsicum and
  parsley. Mix well.
4 Spoon filling into shells.
  Sprinkle with breadcrumbs.
  Bake 15 minutes OR microwave on Medium for 5 minutes. Serve hot.

CHEESY CORN POTATOES

4 medium potatoes
⅔ cup coarsely grated
  Cheddar cheese
130 g can creamed corn
1 tablespoon chopped chives

1 Turn oven to 210°C (415°F).
  Pierce potatoes. Place on
  oven rack. Bake 1 hour OR
  microwave on High for 10
  minutes.
2 Cut potatoes in half, scoop
  out flesh. Arrange potato
  shells on oven tray.
3 Mash scooped-out potato in
  a bowl. Add cheese, corn
  and chives. Mix well.
4 Spoon filling into shells.
  Bake 15 minutes OR
  microwave on Medium 5
  minutes. Serve hot.

When potatoes are cooked, cut in half. Cool slightly.

Scoop out flesh with a spoon. Mix with filling.

Cook mince until all red is gone. Stir to break up lumps.

CHAPTER FIVE

DESSERTS AND CAKES

Luscious sweet things to make and enjoy! In this chapter you'll find puddings and cakes, pikelets, trifles, and two types of ice-cream. For a really fun dessert try our White Chocolate Fondue with fresh fruit.

ROCKY ROAD ICE-CREAM

Serves 6

100 g packet red glacé cherries
100 g packet coloured marshmallows
¼ cup choc bits
¼ cup crushed nuts

2 tablespoons desiccated coconut
1 L vanilla ice-cream, softened
60 g dark chocolate, chopped

This ice-cream makes a great sundae. Fill a long glass with a scoop of rocky road, sliced bananas, more ice-cream, top with Chocolate Fudge Sauce (page 71).

1 Chop cherries finely.

2 Cut marshmallows into pieces.

3 Put cherries, marshmallows, choc bits, nuts and coconut in a big bowl.

4 Add ice-cream. Mix gently.

5 Pour into a loaf or bread tin. Smooth the top.

6 Cover with plastic wrap. Put in freezer for 3 hours.

7 Melt dark chocolate in a bowl over hot water.

8 Spoon melted chocolate over ice-cream and serve.

CREAMY APRICOT RICE

Serves 4

425 g can apricot halves
540 g can vanilla-flavoured
  rice cream
1 teaspoon grated orange
  rind

1¼ cups thickened cream
2 tablespoons icing sugar
2 tablespoons slivered
  almonds, toasted

Think of ways to make the food you cook look great. Serve this dessert in your prettiest glasses.

1
Drain all the liquid from apricots. Chop finely.

2
Put apricots and rice cream into a big bowl. Add 1 teaspoon rind. Mix gently.

3
Put cream and sugar in a small bowl. Beat until firm peaks form.

4
Put ½ the cream onto the rice. Mix through very gently.

5
Spoon into pretty glasses.

6
Put in fridge for 1 hour.

7
Top with the rest of the cream.

8
Sprinkle with almonds. Serve immediately.

STRAWBERRY BOMBE ALASKA

Serves 4-6

1 plain sponge cake
500 mL vanilla ice-cream,
  softened
2 tablespoons strawberry
  ice-cream topping

2 egg whites
¼ cup caster sugar
1 tablespoon flaked
  almonds

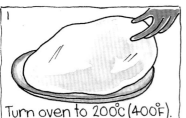

1 Turn oven to 200°c (400°F). Line a pizza tray with foil.

2 Cut cake in half. Put bottom half on tray.

3 Put ice-cream and topping in a bowl. Mix well.

4 Spoon ice-cream onto middle of cake. (Leave 2cm around edge.) Put top on.

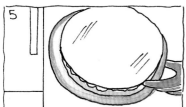

5 Put in freezer for 1 hour or until very firm.

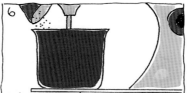

6 Put egg whites in a clean bowl. Beat until stiff, slowly adding sugar.

7 Spread meringue evenly over cake. Sprinkle with almonds.

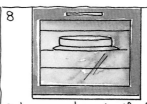

8 Put on centre shelf of oven. Bake for 3-5 minutes. Serve immediately.

WHITE CHOCOLATE FONDUE

Makes 1½ cups

100 g packet white marshmallows
125 g white chocolate
½ cup sweetened condensed milk
⅓ cup sour cream
1 teaspoon imitation vanilla essence
fresh fruit, for dipping

1 Cut marshmallows into small pieces.

2 Chop chocolate coarsely.

3 Put condensed milk in a small pan. Heat gently for 5 minutes.

4 Add marchmallows. Stir until almost smooth.

5 Add chocolate. Take pan off heat.

6 Beat until chocolate melts and sauce is smooth.

7 Add cream and vanilla. Stir gently.

8 To serve, put the sauce in a bowl. Dip fruit in and eat.

CHOC-HONEYCOMB MOUSSE

Serves 4

½ cup thickened cream
250 g milk chocolate, chopped
¼ cup sugar
2 teaspoons gelatine
½ cup water
2 x 35 g chocolate-coated honeycomb bars, chopped

1 Heat cream gently in a small pan.

2 Add chocolate. Take off heat and stir until chocolate melts.

3 Pour into mixing bowl. Put aside to cool.

4 Mix sugar, gelatine and water in a small pan. Stir until sugar dissolves.

5 Turn up heat and boil. Take off heat and pour into mixing bowl.

6 Beat on Medium speed 10 minutes until thick and fluffy.

7 Gently mix chocolate through. Spoon mousse into 4 dishes.

8 Put in fridge for 30 minutes. Sprinkle honeycomb over and serve.

BLUEBERRY PIKELETS

Makes about 16

1 cup self-raising flour
2 tablespoons caster sugar
1 teaspoon grated lemon
 rind
1 egg, lightly beaten
⅓ cup sour cream
¼ cup milk
1 cup fresh blueberries
1 teaspoon oil
½ cup maple syrup

1. Sift flour into a mixing bowl. Stir in sugar and rind.

2. Add egg, cream and milk.

3. Beat until mixture is smooth, with no lumps.

4. Add 2 tablespoons of blueberries. Stir gently.

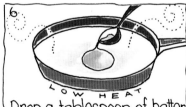

5. Brush a non-stick fry pan with oil. Heat until warm.

6. Drop a tablespoon of batter in. Shape into a circle about 8cm wide.

7. Cook 2 minutes; turn and cook other side 2 minutes until golden.

8. Serve with blueberries piled on. Pour maple syrup over.

Make pikelet batter the day before, cover bowl with plastic wrap and place in fridge. A good idea if you are cooking them for breakfast, because you don't have to get up so early.

PINEAPPLE CREAM TRIFLE

Serves 6

85 g packet lemon
  jelly crystals
1 cup boiling water
250 g packet jam
  sponge roll
⅓ cup custard powder

1 cup milk
450 g can crushed
  pineapple, well drained
1¼ cups thickened cream
2 tablespoons icing sugar

Trifles are a great way to use up bits and pieces. Any left-over cake will do as the base; use raspberry jelly and tinned peaches for a different flavour.

1

Put jelly and water in a small bowl. Stir until jelly dissolves.

2

Cut jam roll into slices. Put on bottom of a serving bowl. (About 25 cm.)

3

Pour jelly over cake.

4

Put custard powder and milk in a small pan. Stir until smooth.

5

Cook, stirring slowly, until custard thickens and boils.

6

Take off heat. Stir in pineapple. Put lid on and leave 5 minutes. Spread over jelly.

7

Put cream and sugar in a small bowl. Beat until thick. Spread over custard.

8

Cover bowl with plastic wrap. Put in fridge for 2–3 hours.

RASPBERRY ROYALE

Serves 4-6

85 g packet raspberry jelly
  crystals
1 teaspoon gelatine
1 cup boiling water
125 g soft cream cheese
1¼ cups thickened cream
½ cup fresh raspberries
250 g packet jam
  sponge roll

1 | Put jelly, gelatine and water in a small bowl. Stir to dissolve.

2 | Put in fridge for 30 minutes.

3 | Put cream cheese and cream in a mixing bowl. Beat 3 minutes on low speed.

4 | Add cool jelly mixture. Beat 3 minutes on medium speed.

5 | Add raspberries. Mix gently.

6 | Cut cake into 1 cm slices. Cover bottom and sides of serving bowl.

7 | Spread raspberry filling on top of cake. Cover with plastic wrap.

Always read the recipe through before you start cooking. Note how long it will take, and work out if you have time to make the dish. Try and plan your cooking well ahead.

8 | Put in fridge overnight. Turn out onto a flat plate to serve.

MANGO ICE-CREAM

Serves 4

2 teaspoons cornflour
2 tablespoons sugar
1 cup cream
1 cup milk
170 g can mango pulp

1. Mix cornflour, sugar and cream in a pan.

2. Add milk. Cook, stirring, until it boils and thickens.

3. Remove from heat. Leave to cool slightly.

4. Stir in mango pulp.

5. Pour mixture into a big plastic bowl. Cover with plastic wrap.

6. Put in freezer 2 hours until the ice-cream hardens a little.

7. Take out and beat on Medium speed 4 minutes.

8. Put in freezer again for 4 hours or until firm.

TROPICAL CARROT LOAF

Makes one 25 cm loaf
1½ cups coarsely grated
   carrot
225 g can pineapple
   pieces, drained
1 teaspoon grated
   orange rind
2 cups wholemeal
   self-raising flour

½ cup oil
3 eggs, lightly beaten
⅔ cup caster sugar
TOPPING
250 g cream cheese,
   softened
1 teaspoon grated
   orange rind
½ cup icing sugar

To decorate cake, draw a carrot shape in the icing with a skewer. Carefully fill in the outline with coloured sprinkles.

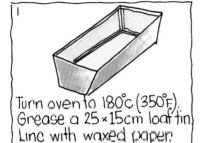

1 Turn oven to 180°c (350°F). Grease a 25×15cm loaf tin. Line with waxed paper.

2 Put carrot, pineapple, rind, flour, oil, eggs and sugar in a big bowl.

3 Mix well with a fork.

4 Spread evenly in tin. Bake for 55 minutes.

5 Turn cake out and cool on a wire rack.

6 Put cream cheese, rind and icing sugar in a small bowl.

7 Beat until light and fluffy.

8 Turn cake right-side up. Spread topping over cake.

LEMON BUTTERFLY CAKES

Makes about 35
340 g packet buttercake
   mix
2 teaspoons grated
   lemon rind
⅔ cup bottled lemon butter
½ cup thickened cream
¼ cup icing sugar
35 silver balls

1. Turn oven to 180°C (350°F). Lay out 35 paper patty cases.

2. Follow directions on packet to make cake batter. Mix in the rind.

3. Put 1 tablespoon batter into each patty case. Bake for 15 minutes. Cool on wire rack.

4. Cut a circle from the top of each cake. Cut circles in half.

5. Put ½ teaspoon lemon butter into each cake.

6. Put cream in a small bowl. Beat until firm peaks form.

7. Put 1 tablespoon cream onto each cake. Press the half-circles on top.

8. Dust with icing sugar. Put a silver ball on top.

STICKY HONEY PECAN RING

Makes one 20 cm ring cake
340 g packet buttercake
  mix
¼ cup sour cream
⅔ cup pecan nuts, finely
  chopped
⅔ cup honey
1 tablespoon lemon juice
whole pecans, to decorate

1

Turn oven to 180°C (350°F).
Grease a 20cm ring tin.

2

Follow directions on packet
to make cake batter.

3

Add sour cream to
batter. Beat well.

4

Add chopped nuts. Mix
in gently.

5

Spread evenly in tin. Bake
for 35 minutes.

6

Put honey and juice in
a small pan. Heat until
just warm.

7

Pour over hot cake in tin.

8

Turn out onto serving plate.
Top with nuts. Serve hot.

DOUBLE CHOCOLATE CAKE

Makes one 23 cm cake

125 g butter, softened
¾ cup caster sugar
2 eggs
1¼ cups self-raising flour
2 tablespoons custard
    powder
⅓ cup cocoa
½ cup water
BUTTERCREAM
125 g butter
1⅓ cups icing sugar sifted
½ cup cocoa
2 tablespoons milk

1 Turn oven to 180°C (350°F). Grease a deep 23 cm round cake tin.

2 Put butter, sugar, eggs, flour, custard powder and cocoa in mixing bowl.

3 Add water. Beat 2 minutes on low speed, then 4 minutes on high speed.

4 Spread evenly in tin. Bake 40 minutes. Turn onto a rack to cool.

5 Put butter, icing sugar, cocoa and milk in a small bowl.

6 Beat 1 minute on low speed, then 4 minutes on high speed.

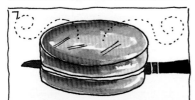

7 Cut cake in half. Spread buttercream on bottom half.

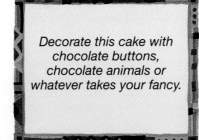

Decorate this cake with chocolate buttons, chocolate animals or whatever takes your fancy.

8 Cover with cake top. Spread buttercream over top and sides.

YUMMY DRINKS

Choc-mint Dream

Fruit Salad Smoothie

Smoothies and shakes are simple to make, look fantastic and are absolutely scrumptious to drink. They only take a minute to prepare and make a great snack or after-school treat. Some of these recipes are almost a meal In themselves! No time for breakfast? Whip up an energy shake!

Feel like some fruit? Try a smoothie loaded with fresh fruit. You'll be getting a taste treat and a vitamin-packed drink that will keep you going all day long.

Whizz these drinks up in your blender and serve them in a big, tall glass. Use your imagination and decorate with coloured sprinkles, little umbrellas, pieces of fruit or whatever you have on hand.

SMOOTHIE CHECKLIST

Collect all the things you will need to make your smoothie.

- Blender
- Ice-cream scoop; rubber or plastic spatula (for scraping mixture out of the blender)
- Ice cubes or ice-cream
- Fruit
- Cold milk
- Flavourings
- Decorations

CHERRY-BERRY SPIDER

Makes 2

4 cherries and 4 blueberries
2 tablespoons raspberry or blackcurrant cordial
2 cups lemonade
2 scoops vanilla ice-cream

1 Put two cherries and two blueberries in each glass.
2 Add 1 tablespoon cordial to each glass.
3 Gently pour on lemonade.
4 Top each glass with a scoop of ice-cream. Decorate with cherries and blueberries.
5 Serve immediately with a spoon and straw.

CHOC-MINT DREAM

Makes 2

4 scoops choc-mint ice-cream
1½ cups milk
chocolate sprinkles

1 Put 2 scoops of ice-cream and milk in blender.
2 Blend until smooth.
3 Pour into tall glasses.
4 Top each glass with a scoop of ice-cream and chocolate sprinkles.
5 Serve immediately with a spoon and straw.

Energy Shake

Melty Malted Smoothie

PINA COLADA SMOOTHIE

Makes 2

1½ cups pineapple juice
1 banana
½ cup canned thick coconut milk
½ cup ice cubes (optional)

1 Put all ingredients in blender.
2 Blend together until smooth.
3 Pour into tall glasses to serve.

MELTY MALTED SMOOTHIE

Makes 2

2 cups milk
2 tablespoons drinking chocolate
2 tablespoons malt powder
2 scoops vanilla ice-cream
1 flaked chocolate bar, cut in half
2 scoops vanilla ice-cream, extra

1 Put milk, chocolate, malt and 2 scoops ice-cream in blender.
2 Blend together until smooth.
3 Pour into 2 big mugs, micro-wave on High 1 minute or until hot.
4 Pour into 2 mugs, top with a scoop of ice-cream and half a chocolate bar.
5 Serve immediately with a spoon.

ENERGY SHAKE

Makes 2

1½ cups skim milk or soy milk
1 tablespoon skim milk powder
½ cup yoghurt
1 tablespoon honey
1 banana
6 strawberries (optional)
cinnamon, to sprinkle

1 Put all ingredients in blender.
2 Blend together until smooth.
3 Pour into tall glasses to serve.
4 Sprinkle a little cinnamon on top.

FRUIT SALAD SMOOTHIE

Makes 2

1½ cups milk
2 scoops vanilla ice-cream
1 cup chopped fruit (passionfruit, strawberries, banana, etc)
½ cup ice-cubes
2 tablespoons honey

1 Put all ingredients in blender.
2 Blend together until smooth.
3 Pour into tall glasses to serve.

CHAPTER SIX

SLICES, COOKIES AND GIFTS

Look through this chapter when you want to
make a little something for afternoon tea, when it's
time to make a contribution to the local cake stall,
or when you just want to make a charming gift for
someone special.

VANILLA SLICE

Serves 6
- 250 g Morning Coffee biscuits
- 2 cups milk
- 1 cup cream
- 85 g packet instant vanilla pudding mix
- 1½ cups icing sugar, sifted
- 2 tablespoons passionfruit pulp
- 60 g butter, melted

1 Line a deep 19cm square cake tin with foil.

2 Arrange a row of biscuits over the bottom.

3 Put milk and cream in a small mixing bowl. Sprinkle pudding mix on top.

4 Beat 5 minutes on medium speed. Pour over biscuits.

5 Top with another layer of biscuits (wrong side up).

6 Beat icing sugar, passionfruit and butter in a small bowl until smooth.

7 Spread over biscuits.

8 Put in fridge overnight before cutting. Cut into 6 slices to serve.

CHEESECAKE SLICE

Makes about 20 slices

85 g packet strawberry
   jelly crystals
1 cup boiling water
60 g butter
125 g dark chocolate,
   chopped
315 g packet plain
   cheesecake mix

1 Line a square cake tin with foil.

2 Put jelly and water in a small bowl. Stir until jelly dissolves.

3 Melt butter gently in a small pan. Add chocolate. Stir until it melts.

4 In a small bowl mix chocolate with biscuit crumbs from cheesecake mix.

5 Press into bottom of tin. Smooth surface.

6 Follow directions on packet to make filling.

7 Spread over biscuit base. Put in fridge for 20 minutes.

8 Top with cooled jelly. Put in fridge 2-3 hours until jelly has set. Cut into squares.

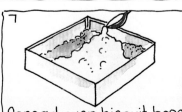

MOCHA WALNUT SLICE

Makes about 16 slices

125 g butter
½ cup milk chocolate melts
3 teaspoons instant coffee
   granules
½ cup caster sugar
1 egg, lightly beaten
1 teaspoon imitation
   vanilla essence
1 cup plain flour
1 cup chopped walnuts

1 Turn oven to 160°c (328°F). Grease a shallow oblong cake tin. Line with baking paper.

2 Melt butter gently in a small pan. Add chocolate. Stir until it melts.

LOW HEAT

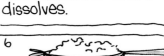

3 Add coffee. Stir until it dissolves.

4 Pour into a big mixing bowl.

5 Add sugar, egg and vanilla. Mix well.

6 Sift flour into bowl. Add walnuts. Mix through gently

7 Spread evenly in tin. Bake 30 minutes.

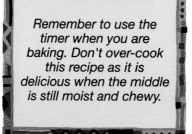

Remember to use the timer when you are baking. Don't over-cook this recipe as it is delicious when the middle is still moist and chewy.

8 Cool in tin. Cut into slices to serve.

CHUNKY CHOCOLATE COOKIES

Makes 16

½ cup brown sugar
1 egg
⅓ cup oil
2 tablespoons cocoa
½ cup self-raising flour
½ cup plain flour
⅓ cup choc bits
60 g white chocolate, chopped

1

Turn oven to 180°C (350°F). Lightly grease 2 biscuit trays.

2
Put sugar, egg and oil in a mixing bowl. Mix well with a fork.

3

Sift cocoa and flours into bowl.

4
Add chocolates. Mix through gently.

5

Knead lightly with hands to make a soft dough.

6

Make balls by rolling 1 tablespoon of dough.

7
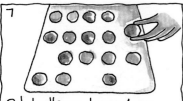
Put balls on tray 4cm apart. Bake 1 tray at a time for 12 minutes.

8

Leave on tray 5 minutes, then cool on wire rack.

CHERRY MACAROONS

Makes 16

½ cup condensed milk
1 cup desiccated coconut
1 cup shredded coconut
100 g packet glacé cherries
1 tablespoon self-raising
   flour
1 tablespoon custard
   powder

1. Turn oven to 180°c (350°F). Lightly grease 2 biscuit trays.

2. Put condensed milk and all coconut in a mixing bowl.

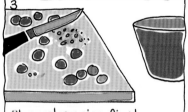
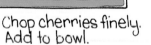

3. Chop cherries finely. Add to bowl.

4. Sift flour and custard powder into bowl.

5. Mix well.

6. Drop tablespoons of mixture onto tray, 4 cm apart.

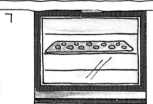

7. Bake one tray at a time on centre shelf for 15 minutes.

8. Leave on trays 5 minutes. Lift off and cool on wire rack.

CRISPY APRICOT BALLS

Makes 18 balls

⅔ cup crushed plain
   biscuit crumbs
1 cup Rice Bubbles
⅓ cup desiccated coconut
250 g white chocolate,
   chopped

1 tablespoon oil
3 tablespoons apricot
   jam
⅔ cup coloured sprinkles

Roll these balls in crushed nuts or desiccated coconut instead of sprinkles if you like.

1 Put biscuit crumbs, Rice Bubbles and coconut in bowl. Mix gently.

2 Melt chocolate in a bowl over hot water.

3 Take off heat. Add oil. Stir until smooth.

4 Put jam in a small pan. Warm gently — don't let it boil.

5 Make a well in centre of crumb mixture.

6 Pour in melted chocolate and jam. Mix gently.

7 Make balls by rolling 1 tablespoon of mixture.

8 Roll balls in sprinkles. Leave to set at room temperature.

CUTOUT CHRISTMAS COOKIES

Makes 12-14 biscuits

125 g butter
⅔ cup icing sugar
1 egg yolk
2 teaspoons imitation
 vanilla essence

2 cups plain flour
1 tablespoon currants

1. Turn oven to 160°C (325°F).

2. Put butter, sugar, egg yolk and vanilla in a small bowl. Beat until light and creamy.

3. Sift flour into bowl. Add currants. Mix to a soft dough.

4. Knead gently on a lightly-floured board. Divide in half.

5. Roll out half the pastry between sheets of baking paper.

6. Roll out thinly. Repeat with other half of pastry. Put in fridge for 20 minutes.

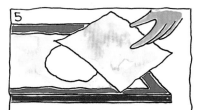

7. Cut dough into shapes. Bake on top shelf for 20 minutes.

Leave on trays 5 minutes. Lift off and cool on wire rack.

COCONUT MARSHMALLOWS

Makes 16

1 cup sugar
1 tablespoon gelatine
¾ cup hot water
½ teaspoon coconut
   essence
1 cup desiccated coconut

1
Line a deep 19 cm square cake tin with foil.

2
Put sugar, gelatine and water in a small pan. Stir 5 minutes.

3
Simmer 5 minutes more without stirring.

4
Turn up heat. Boil without stirring for 5 minutes more.

5
Take pan off heat. Leave for 5 minutes, then beat for 5 minutes. Stir in essence.

6
Spread marshmallow evenly in tin. Leave for 1 hour until firm.

7
Put coconut in pan. Heat gently until golden. Take off heat and cool.

8
Cut marshmallow in squares and toss in coconut. Wrap brightly.

BANANA BITES

Makes about 10

2 medium bananas
125 g milk chocolate melts
1 teaspoon oil
½ cup chocolate sprinkles

1. Peel bananas. Cut off ends.

2. Cut into 3cm slices.

3. Melt chocolate in a bowl over hot water.

4. Take off heat. Add oil. Stir until smooth.

5. Spread sprinkles on a sheet of greaseproof paper.

6. Using a skewer, dip banana into chocolate.

7. Roll banana in sprinkles.

8. Stand on greaseproof paper. Leave to set at room temperature.

CHOC-CHERRY SPIDERS

Makes 20
100 g packet glacé cherries
⅓ cup flaked almonds, toasted
100 g packet fried egg noodles
200 g dark chocolate, chopped
30 g butter

Chop cherries finely.

Put in a bowl with almonds and noodles.

Melt chocolate and butter in a small bowl over hot water.

Take off heat. Stir until smooth.

Add chocolate to cherry mix. Stir gently to combine.

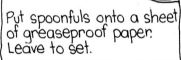

Put spoonfuls onto a sheet of greaseproof paper. Leave to set.

Dust with icing sugar.

Wrap in cellophane and tie with ribbon.

PECAN TARTS

Makes 8

8 frozen shortcrust
 pastry cases
¼ cup self-raising flour
½ teaspoon mixed spice
⅔ cup chopped pecan nuts
1 egg, lightly beaten
1 tablespoon milk
2 tablespoon golden syrup
½ teaspoon imitation
 vanilla essence

1 Turn oven to 190°c (375°F).
Arrange tart cases on
an oven tray.

2 Sift flour and spice into
a mixing bowl.

3 Add nuts. Stir to mix. Make
a well in the centre.

4 Add egg, milk, golden
syrup and vanilla.

5 Beat with a fork until
almost smooth.

6 Spoon filling evenly
into tarts.

7 Bake on top shelf 15
minutes. Cool on a rack.

8 Put in little boxes, wrap
in cellophane and tie
with ribbon.

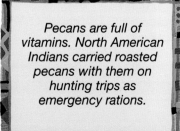

*Pecans are full of
vitamins. North American
Indians carried roasted
pecans with them on
hunting trips as
emergency rations.*

USEFUL INFORMATION

The recipes in this book are all thoroughly tested,
using standard metric measuring cups and spoons.
All cup and spoon measurements are level.
We have used eggs with an average weight of 60 g each
in all recipes.

WEIGHTS AND MEASURES

In this book, metric measures
and their imperial equivalents
have been rounded out to the
nearest figure that is easy to
use. Different charts from
different authorities vary
slightly; the following are the
measures we have used
consistently throughout our
recipes.

OVEN TEMPERATURE CHART

	°C	°F
Very slow	120	250
Slow	150	300
Mod Slow	160	325
Moderate	180	350
Mod Hot	210	425
Hot	240	475
Very Hot	260	450

LENGTH

Metric	Imperial
5 mm	¼ in
1 cm	½ in
2 cm	¾ in
5 cm	2 in
8 cm	3 in
10 cm	4 in
12 cm	5 in
15 cm	6 in
20 cm	8 in
25 cm	10 in
30 cm	12 in
46 cm	18 in
50 cm	20 in
61 cm	24 in

CUP AND SPOON MEASURES

A basic metric cup set consists
of 1 cup, ½ cup, ⅓ cup and
¼ cup sizes.

The basic spoon set
comprises 1 tablespoon,
1 teaspoon, ½ teaspoon and
¼ teaspoon.

1 cup	250 mL/8 fl oz
½ cup	125 mL/4 fl oz
⅓ cup (4 tablespoons)	80 mL / 2½ fl oz
¼ cup (3 tablespoons)	60 mL/2 fl oz
1 tablespoon	20 mL
1 teaspoon	5 mL
½ teaspoon	2.5 mL
¼ teaspoon	1.25 mL

LIQUIDS

Metric	Imperial
30 mL	1 fl oz
60 mL	2 fl oz
100 mL	3½ fl oz
125 mL	4 fl oz (½ cup)
155 mL	5 fl oz
170 mL	5½ fl oz (⅔ cup)
200 mL	6½ fl oz
250 mL	8 fl oz (1 cup)
300 mL	9½ fl oz
375 mL	12 fl oz
410 mL	13 fl oz
470 mL	15 fl oz
500 mL	16 fl oz (2 cups)
600 mL	1 pt (20 fl oz)
750 mL	1 pt 5 fl oz (3 cups)
1 litre (1000 mL)	1 pt 12 fl oz (4 cups)

DRY INGREDIENTS

Metric	Imperial
15 g	½ oz
30 g	1 oz
45 g	1½ oz
60 g	2 oz
75 g	2½ oz
100 g	3½ oz
125 g	4 oz
155 g	5 oz
185 g	6 oz
200 g	6½ oz
250 g	8 oz
300 g	9½ oz
350 g	11 oz
375 g	12 oz
400 g	12½ oz
425 g	13½ oz
440 g	14 oz
470 g	15 oz
500 g	1 lb (16 oz)
750 g	1 lb 8 oz
1 kg (1000 g)	2 lb

GLOSSARY

capsicum = sweet pepper
cornflour = cornstarch
flour = use plain all purpose
    unless otherwise
    specified
eggplant = aubergine
spring onion = shallot
zucchini = courgettes

INDEX

Front cover, Chocolate Fudge Sauce (p. 71) served with vanilla ice-cream (top) and Hot Bean Dogs (p. 14). Inside front cover, Strawberry Bombe Alaska (p. 80).

Left, Pina Colada Smoothie (p. 93) and Cherry-berry Spider (p. 92). Back cover, Raspberry Royale (p. 86).

Published by Murdoch Books, a division of Murdoch Magazines Pty Ltd
213 Miller Street, North Sydney, NSW 2060

Murdoch Books Food Editor: Jo Anne Calabria
Recipe Development: Voula Mantzouridis
Editor: Rosalie Higson
Design and Finished Art: Jayne Hunter
Photography: Andrew Furlong
Recipe Illustrations: Jayne Hunter
Food Stylist: Georgina Dolling
Food Stylist's Assistant: Jodie Vassallo
Border Illustrations: Jan Gosewinckel

Publisher: Anne Wilson
Publishing Manager: Mark Newman
Production Manager: Catie Ziller
Managing Editor: Susan Tomnay
Art Director: Lena Lowe
Marketing Manager: Mark Smith
National Sales Manager: Keith Watson
Project Co-ordinator: Kerrie Ray

National Library of Australia Cataloguing-in-Publication Data
Kids' cookbook 2.
Includes index.
ISBN 0 86411 323 4.

1. Cookery – Juvenile literature. I. title Kids' cookbook two.

641.5123

First published 1993
Printed by Toppan Printing Co. Ltd, Singapore
Typeset by Adtype, Sydney

© Murdoch Books 1993

Distribution in the UK by Australian Consolidated Press (UK) Ltd
20 Galowhill Road, Brackmills, Northampton NN4 OEE.
Enquiries – 0604 760456